Busy Book of Search and Find:
Amazing Animals

Published by Sellers Publishing, Inc.
Copyright © 2021 Sellers Publishing, Inc.
Illustrations © 2021 Collaborate Agency
All rights reserved.

Sellers Publishing, Inc.
161 John Roberts Road, South Portland, Maine 04106
Visit our website: www.sellerspublishing.com
E-mail: rsp@rsvp.com

Charlotte Cromwell, Production Editor

ISBN 13: 978-1-5319-1483-7

10 9 8 7 6 5 4 3 2 1

Printed in China.

Busy Book of Search and Find: Amazing Animals

illustrated by Gema Galán

SELLERS
PUBLISHING

 Giant Tortoise

 Albacore Tuna

Bigeye Tuna

 Irrawaddy Dolphin

 Sea Turtle

UNDER THE SEA!

Below the surface of the waves it's a real party! In the ocean's warmer waters you'll find dolphins and turtles, octopuses, jellyfish, sharks and so much more. They say we know less about the ocean than we do about outer space, which explains why some sea creatures look so alien! There are plenty of endangered creatures in the ocean, which need protection from human activity and the changing climate.

Can you spot these fishy friends in their watery wonderland?

Great White Shark

Whale Shark

Galápagos Penguin

Common Bottlenose Dolphin

Marine Iguana

Sel Whale

Humphead Wrasse

Plains Bison

Swift Fox

Jaguar

Pronghorn

OUT IN THE OPEN

Grasslands exist in many different parts of the globe and they have different names depending on where they are, like prairies, moors, pampas, and steppes! They provide food and shelter to animals such as foxes and ferrets, pronghorns and pangolins! These animals face a variety of threats like poaching and invasive species, and their habitat is often built over by humans.

Can you spot the different animals hiding out in the long grasses?

 Greater Sage-Grouse

 Black-footed Ferret

 Mountain Plover

 Pangolin

How many birds can you find?

 Greater One-Horned Rhino

 African Elephant

SUNNY SAVANNAH

The sprawling grasslands in Africa are host to some of the most magnificent animals on Earth: elephants, rhinos, zebras, lions and so many more! The grass keeps on re-growing no matter how much animals munch on it – it's like an all-you-can-eat buffet! However, lots of the savannah is now being turned into farmland to grow food for humans, making it harder for wildlife to survive.

See if you can spot the animals who live in the tall grasses of the savannah.

 Black Rhino

 Savanna Elephant

African Wild Dog

How many penguins can you find?

Arctic Wolf

Arctic Fox

CHILLING ON ICE!

The Arctic and Antarctic polar regions are beautiful places filled with glaciers and vast expanses of ice. Amazingly, these frigid regions are home to all kinds of polar wildlife. Small communities of people live here too! Even though the extreme cold is a harsh environment for most humans, for polar bears, seals, orcas, penguins and many more animals it's the perfect place! But as the average global temperature increases, ice melts. This disrupts the ecological balance that polar animals depend upon for survival.

Can you spot the endangered animals whose icy homes need to be protected?

Southern Rock-Hopper Penguin

Polar Bear

Penguin

 Macaw

 Black Spider Monkey

 Orangutan

 Sumatran Elephant

 Poison Dart Frog

AMAZING RAINFOREST

In the tropical forests, everything is alive. Frogs hop along the forest floor, while monkeys swing through the trees, and colorful macaws sail and swoop above the canopy. Tread carefully, because you might come across some much bigger creatures like a gorilla or maybe even an elephant! The rainforest is home to so many rare and endangered creatures, but it's disappearing fast.

Can you spot the forest-dwelling animals hiding in the trees?

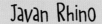
Javan Rhino

Sumatran Rhino

Sloth

Bornean Orangutan

Sumatran Orangutan

Eastern Lowland Gorilla

How many fish can you find?

Leatherback Turtle

Hawksbill Turtle

Staghorn Corals

UNDERWATER CITIES

Coral reefs are a colorful paradise, bustling with a massive variety of marine wildlife. In fact, there are almost as many different life forms living in and around coral reefs as there are in the Amazon Rainforest! Coral reefs are life-sustaining natural wonders, but they are suffering because of warming sea temperatures, pollution, and other man-made threats.

Can you spot the endangered creatures that depend upon coral reefs for their well being?

Green Turtle

Elkhorn

Dugong

How many fish can you find?

Hippopotamus

Indus River Dolphin

Sunda Tiger

16

SWAMPY SEARCH

You might think dolphins only live in the sea, but there are many that live in rivers and lakes close to land, such as the Amazon River Dolphin, which is a surprising shade of pink! The wetlands of the world are a haven to wildlife, and they also form a great spot for migrating birds to stop and take a break on their journey. Many animals rely on this habitat for survival, so it's important that wetlands are protected and respected.

Can you find the different types of endangered species living in the wetlands?

Ganges River Dolphin

Amazon River Dolphin

Yangtze Finless Porpoise

Vaquita

Fin Whale

Beluga Whale

Sea Lion

North Atlan
Right
Whale

SUPER COLD SEA LIFE

The cold oceans are where you'll find most of the planet's largest marine animals, including many types of whale. But don't be scared by their size, because whales are incredibly gentle and kind by their nature. Graceful narwhals are like the real-life unicorns of the ocean! And where there's ice, you'll also find seals and sea lions diving for fish. But people use these waters for fishing too, which can make it hard for ocean wildlife to survive.

Can you spot the marine animals in their chilly habitat?

Bluefin Tuna

Hector's Dolphin

Seal

Bowhead Whale

Narwhal

Blue Whale

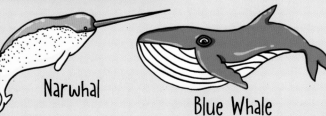
Pacific Salmon

Gray Whale

How many birds can you find?

 Tree Kangaroo

 Snow Leopard

MIGHTY MOUNTAINS

Mountains can be host to all different types of amazing plants and animals, because the temperature changes rapidly as you go higher, getting colder and colder. At lower levels you might find tree-dwelling animals like pandas or kangaroos, but up high where there is snow and ice, you're more likely to see a snow leopard or two. Lots of people live on mountains, so they need to build roads and buildings, which can destroy the local ecosystem.

Can you spot the endangered creatures who share their mountain home?

Amur Leopard

Giant Panda

Mountain Gorilla

Cross River Gorilla

Chimpanzee

Continental Tiger

Saola

Bonobo

Borneo Pygmy Elephant

WELCOME TO THE JUNGLE

Eighty percent of the earth's plant and animal species live in the world's forests. There are tigers, apes, elephants and jaguars! Everywhere you go is teeming with wildlife, like weird mushrooms and vibrant flowers! The huge number of different life forms is what's called biodiversity. It means that to protect the endangered animals, we have to protect their homes and food sources too.

Can you find the endangered creatures roaming in the jungle?

Forest Elephant

Jaguar

Sri Lankan Elephant

Pangolin

Asian Elephant

Indian Elephant

Western Lowland Gorilla

How many insects can you find?

 Continental Tiger

 Giant Panda

INTO THE WOODS

Temperate forests have a diverse range of wildlife. In temperate forests you'll find hedgehogs, foxes, beavers, owls and BEARS, among others! Sometimes woodlands are cleared to make room for development, threatening the animals that lived within them. Thankfully there are lots of people working hard to protect and regrow this beautiful green habitat.

Can you spot the animals that live within the woodlands?

 Red Panda

 Brown Bear

 Monarch Butterfly

Answers

Hidden animals are highlighted in red.

UNDER THE SEA!

OUT IN THE OPEN

SUNNY SAVANNAH

AMAZING RAINFOREST

SWAMPY SEARCH

INTO THE WOODS